The Casting Boat

John Lindley

HEADLAND

First published in 2009
by
HEADLAND PUBLICATIONS
38 York Avenue
West Kirby, Wirral
CH48 3JF

British Library Cataloguing in Publication Data.
A full CIP record for this book is available from the British Library
ISBN
978 1 902096 59 9

HEADLAND acknowledges the financial
assistance of Arts Council England

The Casting Boat

Tell all the Truth but tell it slant
Emily Dickinson

CONTENTS

CONTENTS *continued*

Start Your Own Parrot

Begin with two small feathers
handed to you by a stranger in the pub perhaps
but begin.
Don't think overmuch about working conditions.
Warm weather, the sound of tropical rain,
strange vegetation and leaves underfoot –
none of this really counts for much.
It's not the detail or even the outcome
but the intent that matters.
It's the starting not the finishing.
There are easier things to do after all,
parts are hard to come by
and instructions less than useless.
Just remember
a fully-plumed macaw is not the aim.
For myself, ending up
with the overhanging half of the beak,
a wingtip and one of those dragon-scaled gloves
for a left or right claw would be enough,
providing I could put them together in some way.
Attempts at parrots are like attempts at art; worthwhile.
No need for justification. The best art speaks for itself.
Of course, the best parrots do too
but one can't have everything.

Ghost Painting

I will paint my house *ghost*
with no relief colour;
interior walls, ceilings, doors,
window frames – all *ghost*.

There will be no preparatory wash
or sand, no undercoat
only the unhurried hush
of dipped bristles whispering *ghost*.

I will draw from a pot
of this grey camouflage,
see each combing stroke
make still paler the putty and plaster,

slick the red, crumb-coated brick
beneath to transparency.
The work will be swift –
each surface side done at a stroke.

I'll watch my hand slip through rooms
like fish through fog
until there are only the ghost veils
of spiders hammocking the corners,

brushes like badly cut hair
dripping *ghost* in a house open to all,
where none dare come.
At a sink anchored to nothing

I'll twist the transparency
of turps between my palms,
gaze through glass suspended in air,
count my fingers back one by one.

The Piano Players

Each night, as if afraid the keys will escape,
she locks the lid before retiring,
seals in all the day's playing
and in darkness under a lacquered sky,
from top to bottom A, all are equal
and even the key that sticks becomes one of the crowd.

Does anything sleep deeper than an instrument unplayed?
Everywhere there must be occasions such as this –
hammers unswung, strings unplucked,
undrawn bows, snug in sealed velvet, sawing only on sleep,
drums taut with expectation, solid body guitars
with sockets yawning the absence of electricity.

And throughout the world, too eager to even dress,
every day is Christmas for the piano players
with their stockinged-feet mornings.
Wide-eyed, they come down to a gift both new and familiar,
night skies of black, cream and mahogany
brightening to seven octaves worth of day.

Out back – 1961

Night-time I have them guard the narrow strip
beyond the window, rifles at the ready;
wake unsurprised to find that some still stand up,
untouched by breeze or touched by sense of duty.

Beyond the plastic soldiers on my sill
I see the shed where the mad dog crept, was killed,
not clean and quick as a mockingbird by
Atticus, but subtly by Authority.

Walk out: the smell of creosote and calm,
the stone cold morning flags becoming warm
underfoot, the taste of forbidden fruit –
the berries I was warned never to eat.

Out here, a foundry of sun on wrought iron chairs,
indistinct territories, vague borders,
a garden overstuffed by a clear -
eyed woman who loved flowers more than order.

Through French windows Dad's cornet silvers the air.
I hear his tongue-tip flutter in the mouth-
piece, hear the Capstan brown of his smoker's breath
between practice notes before *Crimond* stirs.

In and Out of Touch

Not long before it was too late
I began to remember to kiss my mother,
to plant one on her cheek firmly
and wetly enough to make up
for all the years I hadn't.
Same now with handshakes
with my brother and hugs for my sister.

I've never done family physical.
I've come to it late. But now I readily clench
and clasp to our comings and goings
part, it's true, due to absences, distances
but part to ground myself, to walk
willingly into what I'm part of,
what I'm scared to be parted from.

Missed the boat with my dad –
thirty seconds dead, my dry lips to his forehead
couldn't have counted for much.
He knew I loved him though;
would have heard it above the noise
of me never saying it.

The Chalk Horse

One day shy of scouring and stabled for years
in that stiff-legged stance
something must have touched
her seahorse snout with restlessness.
The dropped rod tail flicked at its tip,
a hoof twitched, a head lifted
and a white mop mane snow-drizzled up from the turf.
An eye once blind and another west gazing
slanted then drilled over a shoulder
and saw, for the first time, a sun heaven-hoisted,
then haunches, back and an entire more than
two hundred year battened-down body
peeled its pasted shape from the earth
and stood shakily, diagonally as a new-born foal
then straightened. One deep bellowing fill
of her long grassed lungs and she was off.
It's said you couldn't see her for chalk dust.

Though some did: at Cherhill and Pewsey,
Marlborough, Devizes and Broad Town
other stamped nags considered the stampede
and were tempted but dozed two-dimensionally on.
Above Uffington, resolutely stylish and content
with his stationary gallop, a cousin stayed fast.
Meanwhile, the betters' favourite, newly-bolted
from Bratton Down, clocked Broad Hinton
and Alton Barnes, flashed her albino flanks at all
she found there and cantered on past kiwi and panda,
the badges of regiments and deep into Dorset.
At Cerne Abbas a wide-eyed spectator,
torn between violence and ecstasy,
considered mounting her and thought better of it,
awaited instead, and unsurprisingly, the next wave
of rolling women on his fifty-foot phallus.

Whether that chalk horse hit the sea and went under
or bleached invisibly against sky or surf
no one knows for sure but by sundown she'd gone
with no credible word of ghost imprint remaining.
What sweat and steam there might have been evaporated.
There's little left now to tell of her moorings:
a scorched hill bereft of white shadow
greening quickly to pasture,
a blown powder trail rapidly scattering.
Of course the vandalism will begin anew.
They have the photographs, the dimensions,
the necessary artistry and geometry to cut her afresh.
They say that this one should stay put.
Stranger things have happened.

The Unmistakable Shapes of Frogs

In death they are themselves
more than any roadkill known.

These flat stars patterning the path,
these smudged wafers in unfinished hop,

these dull-coloured cut-outs, steamrollered dead
are, for all their dark anchorings,

rhinestones in a copper bracelet,
markers on uncharted seas,

paper-light sprites waiting to be flipped and freed
by a wind that can't blow them fat

but can cartwheel these matt-black acrobats
to living, leaping life again.

Joining the Dots

On bad days
the shading is beyond her,
it's more than she can do
to pick up the day's crayon
never mind colour the hours in.

She counts it a success if she can join the dots,
get her head around each number in order
like wire around markers
that peg out her movements.

When it works she circuits the shape,
dot to sequential dot,
bathroom – wardrobe – kitchen – bus,
navigating the jagged outline
of a puzzling programme.

On better days she almost wears its shape,
inhabits its angular territory
and looks both inside and out.

On better days still
she sketches in the details,
finds the palette, colours in.

On bad days don't bother her,
she's busy joining up the dots,
shop – wake – travel – dress,
trying to work out how you can finish
at a starting point, trying to remember
how to get there.

Carry on Listening

give us a one level town
circled by green
give us unspecial needs
give us access all areas
a wheelchair wide world
as easy as yours
slopes and ramps and gentle contours
slight inclines and smooth edges
bear us no grudges
give us hoists and lifts don't
give us shifty looks
give us a pointed finger free zone
give us poems in Braille and Makaton
and the time to read and speak them
give us eye level windows to see through
and new experience to feel through
give us the facts
give us eye contact
our own voice
our freedom of choice
a fair deal
an even keel
give us a level playing field
and when we've worn out those clichés one by one
when all's said but not done
when we're off and doing
out and about
give us clout
give us time
give us space
give us only what *you* wanted
what you take for granted
give us only what you have
given yourselves
a part in life's dance
give us more than just a second's glance
give us a chance

Imprints

On one of those gone Galilean days
St. Peter grasped God's latest word
when he grasped a John Dory,
spilled a gold coin from its mouth
and returned the fish refashioned to the sea,
his dark stain fingerprints on its olive green flanks.

Seems it was ever thus: since The Maker
first hushed a bawling babe, not with a shush
but with a huge forefinger made small
pressed just above the unquivering lip
we have stilled our cries
and become strangely impressionable.

Did Godly fingernails trench two worry lanes
above the bridge of the nose? Did His thumb
prise open the peach of woman and let each
generation poke its head through?

Some would have it so. Myself, I walk
my days in wonder at my unquestioning self;
accept the gracefully shaped sole of my foot
without a thought and know I am the architect
of my own ploughed brow whenever I choose
to ponder each dimple or dent
others claim Heaven-sent.

Picture though, God in his infancy,
play-doughing His templates in clay of us all,
grooving into being – as neatly as the handles of Colts –
the ribs of our chests, lathering and sculpting
our ears' interiors just so, adding that distinctive kink
to heart-shaped hearts and firing them.

Missed Chance

Of all my small regrets
the one I remembered today
had to do with never sending,
as a boy, for those X-Ray Spex.

Of all the temptations that called
from the pages of U.S. comics –
the pen that shot ink,
the fake turds and blood clots –

nothing in those mail order ad's
suggested more possibilities to a lad
than glasses to see through walls,
see through clothes, see through flesh.

Perhaps, even at eleven,
I could see through them
without ordering, see through
the lie, the trick, the con.

Someone told me it was done
with plucked feathers and plastic
and today, in a field,
I see the grey skeleton of a hare,

think of a feather's ribs
and believe it all possible.
No amount of squinting though
is enough to render decades

of memory's walls suddenly transparent
or conjure up Janet Finch's
small breasts, quietly erupting
under a grey school blouse.

By Way of a Change

"I invented the colour of the vowels! – A black, E white, I red, O blue, U green." Arthur Rimbaud

I am walking on my Magritte feet
towards the Milky Way.
White Rabbit late, it took me hours
to thread these laces through my arches,
longer still to get used to the feel
of tarmac beneath my naked toes.

Walking on my Magritte feet
I stand out in the crowd.
People point, raise umbrellas
as if expecting a sudden downpour
of men in suits
and I walk between them,
imagining what surprise
on an everyday Saturday tastes like.

The Milky Way meanwhile
is acrylic on canvas,
dangerously reminiscent of female genitalia.
Freud might interpret my approach as regression –
he had an answer for everything;
everything that is except for the Magritte feet
I'm using to get me there,
everything except the day's synaesthesia
and the black, red and white, white, white
of my walking.

Shaking Hands

no need any more to spit
        before hand
to hand contact to seal
        a contract
really no need
        indeed
now I'm out of
        the suit
and the shine and the ties
        that bind
for contracts at all
        in fact
but still I like the charm
        of it
the fit of clasped palm
        hooked thumbs
the perfect symmetry –
       you/me –
opposing right to extended right
        feels right
and even the southpaw
        ignores
his condition to embrace my hand –
        tradition

Medicine House

for Alan and Griselda Garner

I don't begin this on a Friday,
stotting like a young deer,
but safely and confidently
on a Saturday afternoon
at a dimly lit desk
to the sound of flies' wings
on a sun-struck window.

The plague comes in on the south wind
so I face a windowless wall,
unbranded with horseshoes,
shattered thunderstones around my desk
and write about the way my spirit walked
when I climbed these stairs,
crossed this room, chose this desk.

I write about it now,
hunched free of the body's back pain
but sheathed in this mortal coil
until I unpeg it, let it drift free,
enable it to see with an eye of faith
what I cannot; let it understand
the **V**s and **M**s of witches' marks
notched behind the beams
of a close timbered house
anxious to put its best face forward,
the duality of light in a portrait,
upturned hearts and lost cobblestones,
a labyrinth in the shape of the wind.

The A-Z of Camels

In truth there was very little training necessary.
The Grand Vizier was not only a literary man
but something of an authority on camel characteristics,
knew at once which had the slouchy qualities of an H,
which the W gait of a fourth from last.

Given the weight of the cargo,
individual speed was of little importance.
Enthusiasm was the chief requirement –
too much and those final vowels
would overtake the early ones,
too little and camel K would drop back
and fall silent just in front of camel N.

Individual strength too
(and here camels are no shirkers)
played a part in the selection.
Fairer for sure had the rules of mathematics
been applied but, of course, that was impossible.
There were not four and a half thousand books per hump,
nor (and history neglects to record such detail)
two thousand two hundred and fifty
if the beasts were bactrian
and anyway, we're into 32 letter alphabets here
with all their implications of decimal points and torn pages
so little of the above might apply.

Yet despite all of those foreign titles,
all of those strange shapes,
I can't fail to picture and pity the like
and equivalent of camel S's elastic webbed feet
sinking shin deep into the sand whilst camel X
would accommodate a wineskin or two with his volumes
and still step sprightly as a pantomime horse.

What a sight they must have been though:
at the head, the crop's pick,
eager and early as Earth's first man
and at the back, sloping bored, the doziest of them all,
his long Z winding behind him like sleep speech
in the dizzy desert air.

"In the 10th century the Grand Vizier of Persia took his entire library with him wherever he went. The 117,000 volume library was carried by camels trained to walk in alphabetical order."

Unbelievable Facts by Geoff Tibballs.

Dreams Imitating Art

No, it's not the one about falling
or the other where we find ourselves naked
in the supermarket or street. It's that dream
nobody seems to have where a history's worth of art
animates itself: Mona Lisa smiling knowingly
behind the window of a local bus, a man with two eyes
on the same side of his head, speaking out of the other
into a mobile phone, a pearl-earringed girl
illuminating a launderette about to close
and the light, corn-yellow and crow-black.

I'd pay good money as an entry fee for dreams
such as those – dreams Rubens-plump, Brueghel-busy
and shadowy as a Seurat Sunday afternoon –
starting each one with a view beneath an arched bridge
over mottled water lilies, ending each with a nightmare
made good: four girls on a streakier bridge,
the three with their backs to me turning to speak,
the fourth, with no mouth, inclined to do the same.

Pub Team

Once a winter's week
we'd rattle our Saturday morning hangovers
in a blue tin van
for this:

a hut with no showers,
a pitch with no grass
and a match with no hope.

On grounds snagged with glass
we kicked out and tracked back.
We man-marked to Jacky's dad's barked
'Get in his shorts'
and rode home
razored with mementoes.

Years on
we relate it all fondly,
roll up trouser legs in the pub
to crescent moon scars –
pictures that tell a thousand stories
or rather one story
told a thousand times.

Before Mother and God

Whether through repentance at the point
of the last eyelid's flutter
we come to this judgement,
or via an earlier mugging by faith
on our own Damascus road
what greater test of our nerve and embarrassment
than to stand, shamefaced before our mothers
in the afterlife, tucking our thin tail
of sins shyly behind us?

What more miserable reunion than this;
this penance before mother and God,
one huge with reprimand and forgiveness,
the other lofty and officious,
checking our credentials like border police?

Lord, whose logic escapes me
(and who fails to exist),
spare me this one humiliation.
Mother, who got there before me
(though there's nowhere to get),
pray, close your eyes to my meantime misdemeanours.
Leave me safe and unscrutinised under His CCTV.
Leave me sinning unseen beneath the socket
of a camera without film.

*Foolish Enough to Have Been a Poet**

Clearly no-one to blame but himself then?
All of those days he could have earned
a dirt under the nails, honest to goodness living,
spent instead lounging in an oversized blouse,
wine and laudanum at his elbow
and fingers black with ink.
He should have got out more –
a garret is no place for one's health
but then nor are walks on the fells
trudged only in bad weather
in cloak and crotch chafing boots.
Presumably consumption - the least he could have expected.
And that, no doubt, coming so soon after the syphilis.
I expect they did right by him at the end:
snuffed out the candle, burnt the letters,
got out the winding sheet.
Better this inscription, I suppose, than chipping a line
of his verse on the headstone –
doubt anyone would have understood a word of it.

** Inscribed, at his own request, on the headstone of Asa Benveniste (1925 – 1990).*

Tricks of Light

Tell us that story again –
the one about seeing stars already dead,
stars cold and extinguished,
stars of blown ash and cinder,
stars no longer there.

Let's have faith in it awhile,
pretend there's some truth to the tale,
tell ourselves seeing isn't believing
and repeat that statement
until we believe that it's true.

Now let's take this counterfeit light
into each star struck iris and blink it away.
Look at the heavens now,
awash with black jackstones
invisible on the same black background;
only the misshapen moon
throwing off a light we can trust.

Then tell us about the light the dead –
the earthbound dead – send us.
Tell us how much of it to keep,
how much to let go,
how much to still believe in.

Missing Children

The children I didn't have
are waiting for me somewhere
in the nowhere and never,
queuing with me at turnstiles and ticket booths.
Before shop windows, they urge me
to prove my wallet-willing love.

At some point
they go into politics or homelessness,
take up arms, die young, old,
acquire honours, traits and faults
and I thank Christ (or the nearest equivalent)
for time saved not disinheriting them;
thank Christ that their invisible imprint on my heart
is just that – invisible. Illusory.

All the same
the children I didn't have
back up their generational ghosts
behind my blocked seeds.
They hang their might-have-been heads
like remaindered clothes on a rack.
They knock around in my dreams some days
but I won't knock around with them.
I grew out of them, the idea of them,
as quickly as they would have their first shoes.

Sometimes I count their unborn heads
and count my blessings.
Sometimes they serpent the word *Daddy*
in my stone deaf ear.

A Man of Letters

In every sense.
Not merely as one who etches
to others in ink on parchment
beneath the irregular orbiting feather,
but in the way each nervous tic shakes
the very alpha, the beta from his being.

As a boy he scrawps the sodden street
on hands and knees, strains to detect the ditch
beneath b for *blindness*,
breathes out the s for *scrofula*,
hears the d drone of *deafness*
on the left side of his head
and begins to sense an order to it all.

As a man the o of his hunger,
the v of the crooked arm he writes with,
the unpronounceable hieroglyphics of a facial scar
all become
grist: *n. grain for grinding*
to the
mill: *n. building containing machinery which grinds.*

From Samuel Johnson's candy floss wig,
from his coat, boots, flesh, bone and marrow
tumble more than just the letter of law, instead
a scattered alphabet of architecture, literature and religion,
science and medicine, chemistry, trade,
poetry and politic falls free.

In glory or in grief,
in play and in prayer, words scarcely fail him
and at the close,
not as mad as necessary to brave life's last adventure,
he braves it just the same: dilutes the prescribed opium
and ceases to be extraordinary,
finds as we all have, or will,
the resolution to death's great mystery
in one defining moment.

Leavings/Returnings

When my sister scattered you
like the wind's feed along the garden
to her son's – your grandson's – memory,
I watched the small genies
of your smoky presence corkscrew and coil,

the needle base of each small tornado
freckling the earth, the head of each warm storm
making for your Derbyshire birthplace,
for the districts of Stockport
or for none of them at all.

Over coffee afterwards we spoke only
of hotels, music and car troubles
and somewhere beyond the café's glass
all or none of you at all
tumbled towards or away from us.

Scant Reward

A poor trade this for charity *with* design,
a worse one still for compassion without:
sixty minutes solace a year
from black flame and furnace
and barely time for the blisters to melt
before he's called back to the place
the Hallelujahs can't reach.

He might have hoped for better.
The leper incident aside, he did his bit
late there at the supper and then in the garden,
delivering on two counts,
kissing goodbye to two lives.

But a poor trade this one –
left scorched, crouched on an eighth of ice
with the biggest part of his destiny
beneath the surface.
A trade worse than silver sunken in a potter's field –
thirty pieces to buy the right to hang
from an olive branch like a teardrop
in a shape that no-one, in years to come,
will dangle from their necks;
no-one will finger-draw
on their shoulders and their heads.

According to Matthew Arnold, St. Brandon saw Judas one Christmas night, five centuries after his death, afloat on an iceberg. Judas had been given one hour a year respite from Hell because he once threw his cloak over a ragged leper.

Clock Ticks

With the tip of her thumb
she counted those dry weeks off
on four planets of the same hand –
Jupiter, Saturn, Mercury, Sun –
twisted a gold band down the last
just wide of the marriage line,
said *four weeks over* over and over
to herself, felt the first red drop
in a drought, studied the spot
where the lifeline stops,
watched shoals of her unborn
queue like unresolved hyphens
on the wedge of her hand.

The 101st Man on the Moon

Somehow it wasn't *that* strange.
Throughout that weightless journey
when the machines did all of the work
and all I had to do was squeeze food from a tube
I'd anticipated oddness, but it was all so familiar.
The simulation had been just too good.

Even my moves were predictable:
the two soft bounces when I'd done with the ladder,
the swing and drive down a lunar fairway,
the Vice Vice Presidential pleasantries
droning in my visor.
I broadcasted pride, cracked jokes,
sent love to family and friends,
collected samples for the hell of it.

At some point I drove that old familiar flag
into that old familiar moon
then snapped the setting Earth
and climbed aboard.
I even knew my heart would miss three beats
in the time it took the ignition to fire,
knew that it *would* fire,
knew that if it didn't
I'd make the six o' clock news in Utah
the late night news in Madrid.

Sins of My Fathers

Because I am an atheist
God continues to punish me,
talks of a Son sent and sacrificed
as if in my service; as if it were my fault.

It's been the same always:
ghosts – God-less or fearing –
claim and adopt me, make me their own,
bequeath their misdemeanours like DNA

and I have achieved much: begun wars,
been butcher king and slave master,
transported my culture and pox to foreign shores
wagging the Empire behind me.

Too late now then to be unpicking
this stitched flag from my sleeve.
My crimes grow international and timeless
and God continues to badger me, throws up

a shame-faced man dressed only in leaves
as my polluter, a woman at his side,
face curtained with hands, as my nemesis.
For them I sin retrospectively time and again.

Nine Lives of the Cat

and though Buddha
offers us more than that
theirs are the lives to crave:
their milk teeth cut
nine times over
and
nine times over
their kitten beginnings,
their curtain climbs
and easy rhymes;
nine lifetimes
of sparrow and shrew
hooked through their barbed
or basking days;
nine lifetimes
of backyard fights, padding nights,
of shadow hugging
and making,
of curling, winding and arching;
nine spans
of primping and preening.
Theirs, in a swoon of catnip,
the one true trip repeated,
theirs the full complement
of symphonies completed,
theirs, in their fur, their finery,
far more
than a thousand and one nights
of perfect binary,
theirs the believable magic,
the bucking of logic,
the nine times table
fully laid and set
for the purr and the spit,
the godly silhouette.

Envy these cats,
these acrobats, feet landing
to eight finales,
envy their hearths and their alleys
for they are the blessed,
the dressed-to-the-nines
gods without equals,
theirs the full told tale,
theirs the eight great sequels.

Crossing Borders

Top-cornered in my bedroom window,
the bleached shadow of a man splitting wood
in a bone-coloured moon.

With no message tonight undeliverable,
with a dry wind from Malawi
coughing through cables and moving in my room,

I marvel at everything; understand all:
how the number seven translates into Chichewa
and back again and is pronounced 'magic',

how my screen is the skin of a tribal drum,
how legends resonate in the bowl behind it,
how the stories quietly chant in Microsoft,

how my modem hums with folklore,
my mouse skitters across borders
and is still at the moment it lures from speakers

the sound of blessings for the sake of the living,
the splash of palm wine and chicken blood
for the sake of the dead.

Nervous in Nairobi

There is no known translatable expression
for the answer I give
to the dazed and dangerous gaze
of the kids in this part of town –
not in Swahili, Urdu
or even post-colonial English.

It is a wordless reply,
a series of brisk and businesslike strides,
a fast scanning eye,
a hand in a jeans' pocket
that denies the notes within.

I have never before chewed gum
quite this confidently
with quite this nonchalance.

Out of the Blue

Days after Katrina
Elvis's uniform made it to shore
as surely as the king himself
never made it to here.

Okay. There was that one touchdown
in Scotland in 1960 when,
with three stripes on his arm
and Priscilla on his mind,
his uniform was the real article,

those two hours of airstrip with screams
and autographs and pressmen
to call 'sir', the way he'd say 'sir'
in service and out.

The arrival in the Mississippi Sound
was no more expected – his overboard khakis
not swimming in, sleeve over mildewed sleeve,
but washed up, shackled to a mannequin
that was as still as his twin.

Reports have the water coloured by oil and rust
but I prefer to think the costume came out
of a river as blue as his Cherokee eyes
and the Scottish blood of an ancestor;
a river as blue as Hawaii,
as blue as a moon.

The costume Elvis wore in the movie G.I. Blues was swept off a destroyed floating casino into the Mississippi by Hurricane Katrina.

Nature

Not what you'd call a mother some days,
not when she's all manga eyes and wistfulness,
underage and virginal,
neat as an A-line skirt,
crisp as a new school blouse,
a knees together, don't talk to strangers,
mind your P's and Q's,
blue-ribboned slice of sugar and spice.

Not what you'd call a mother some days,
not when she's the wolf in the red hood,
the bully in the bike shed,
the girl in the bus shelter
with the gum and the aerosol,
the hand job for the businessman
for the price of strong cider.

Not what you'd call a mother some days,
grown up and out of patience
she demands to be heard,
lashes out at the world,
orphans us all by her rage or indifference,
exclaims *Tsunami! Tsunami!*
Who are you to call me names?
Baptises her children.
Christens them 'Dead'.
Christens them 'Missing'.

Identity

Perhaps flat Manc' vowels
bubble beneath the surface of the Ship Canal,
Belfast brogue filters through the estuary,
Brum comes up from the 'Shroppie'
and hard Scouse consonants
wash from The Mersey as silt
but here it's all rinsed into something other –
other than even Birkenhead and Bebington,
Chester and Childer.

A speech born in marl,
fashioned in clay,
caked in coal,
greased by oil
and smelted as ore
speaks of its birthday –
remembers the stove pipe hats,
the high timbered ships,
the knuckles and spades
that cut the link from the Mersey to the Dee,
that dug for an idea
and uncovered an identity

and what was river speak, sea talk,
Northern dialect and Cheshire tongue
is now an accent blasted from phenol
and buffed by a bar of three-penny soap
into the lyric of the land,
the lilt of the sea,
the patter of the Port.

One Dying Shot

To me it *always* seemed believable for the iris
to clasp the last living look as tightly
as the claw of a gold band pins a bloodstone:

the stooped surgeon unclipping the drip
from the pale papyrus over the vein,
the concerned and distant relative

with a will ticking in his head,
the 'ran right out in front of me' man
against a backdrop of grazed sky.

The morgues must be filled with such records –
albums of those whose dim globes gazed heavenwards
at the close before rolling back in their heads.

So now, before the worm drills the lens
or the vitreous humor melts to ash,
before the eye bobs like a cork in formalin,

we have the unnamed killer's face
in a captured snap, Kilroying above a fringed lid,
we have the retina's anagram – Brownie quaint

and digital clear – developed deep in the onion eye,
blazing the surface, too bright to see,
too fantastic to record,

too unthinkable to think of as true;
the unswivelled image of life's last posing,
speckling out of saline, dot by disputed dot.

The The Poems

They are everywhere, unavoidable, tough to resist.
De La Mare has listened to them,
Hardy's maid been ruined by them.
They burst from gaols in Reading,
make their home in Shallot and Innisfree,
lead a menagerie of donkeys, tygers,
thought-foxes, pussycats and owls
down a road not taken.

What is a brigade's charge or a wedding at Whitsun
without them. A soldier is apt to follow them
and Hiawatha sang a bloody song for them.
They are as old as mariners, as passionate as shepherds
yet their portent is as black as a raven,
as gloomy as a darkling thrush.
And oh! what a nuisance they are.
The flea of them infests even Heaven's hounds.

Sometimes we punish them,
put them in their place, send them to the back,
corrupt them into Daffodils, The
but more often we give them their head,
let them clog up our indexes with their interminable stutter.
They are well versed in it; well practised in their art.
They have it down to a
T.

Useless Things

I can't throw away the useless things:
the hinged box
after silk gives up its oyster of ring,

the cheap and vacant plastic cases
that once held
skewed or broken sunglasses,

the slim rectangular boxes
where pens lay
in velvet trenches or indents gripped watches.

For years on end I store these husks
without reason.
I can't explain. Don't even ask.

Hans Christian Andersen's Debt to His Mother and Father

Because of his doubts my feet are as large as a cobbler's sign
Because of her faith narcissism conquers all

Because of her faith I have the high singing voice of an angel
Because of his doubts rough boys tear my trousers, check my sex

Because of his doubts I am dyslexic
        dut have ton yet bene givn the werd too sae so
Because of her faith I can sew the rags of myth
        into visible robes and speak of them

Because of his doubts sexual love is beyond me
Because of her faith sexual love is beyond me

Because of his doubts I am as vain as red shoes
Because of her faith I'm forgiven my dance above my station

Because of his doubts I am moved by love's mawkishness
Because of her faith I visit brothels
        and nothing rises in me but the sap of stories

Because of his doubts he has three drilled holes in his arm
        where God has made him pay
Because of her faith she has the thirst of a mermaid
        yet God forgives her, lets her die for Him

Make No Grave Mistake

"I only seem dead.": Hans Christian Andersen

He wears a note to say he's not expired
and although he dreams of a prince's kiss,
a far lighter brush is all that's required
to stir him: angel's wings, enchanted mists,
red shoes, mermaids, the sound of snow on snow,
a child as tiny as a mother's thumb,
a young girl dying in a match's glow,
invisible silks and a soldier's drum.
He journeys with a rope when he awakens,
and fears the fire that stalks him as he goes,
but in sleep he fears he'll be mistaken
for dead, so clasps the note inside his clothes,
lies on his back, tucks one leg under him,
imagines ballerinas, hearts of tin.

Certainties

blondes play brass
brunettes play violins
from time immemorial
that's the way it's always been
just as yin needs yang
and tonic needs gin
blondes play brass
brunettes play violins

blondes mouth metal
brunettes stroke strings
it's not just the bee
and the nettle that stings
it's not even over
when the fat lady sings
but blondes mouth metal
and brunettes stroke strings

blondes press valves
brunettes draw bows
it's the way it's meant to be
the way it always goes
we all reap the harvest
that the saboteur sows
but blondes press valves
and brunettes draw bows

rivers get fatter
the ozone layer thins
wool turns to water
and a Cheshire Cat grins
trends go out of fashion
others come in
still blondes play brass
brunettes play violins

like the white of the snow
and the green of the grass
like the Jew at the synagogue
the Catholic at Mass
this has been the outcome
this has come to pass
brunettes play violins
blondes play brass

some vicars swear oaths
some sinners sing hymns
there's little you can bet on
with any certainty you'll win
but the sun still rises
and the earth still spins
and blondes play brass
brunettes play violins

sure as eggs wear shells
and bones wear skin
when a wall needs tumbling
the horns come in
when something is burning
a fiddle begins
blondes play brass
brunettes play violins

When Death Knew Its Place

How did so few of us turn out dead back then?
Bar a mate in a bad luck passenger seat,
Kit's baby, who didn't come out right,
pretty much everyone survived my teens.

Or so it seems, penned in by the blessed thing
now, embroiled in the choice of black tie or fawn
to strike the proper tone, do the done thing
at wakes where we celebrate instead of mourn.

I preferred it back then when we kept death
in a box in the corner of the room,
when dying was believable as myth –
just statistics, locations, all of them

rolled out at nine o' clock, by ten past done:
two on the Falls Road, nine more in Saigon.

10 Games to Play with Masks

1

Pick a mask.
Any mask.
Look at it.
Put it back anywhere.
Remember
the mask you first thought of.
All will be revealed.

2

There is a face
beneath
one of these three masks.
When they stop moving
say which.
Go to the back
if you're wrong.

3

Here are two pieces of string.
Thread each one through
the eye sockets of a mask.
Tie them at the back.
Without
tearing the bridge of the nose
pull a face through.

4

Think of the longest
most unpronounceable word
you know.
Say it aloud.
Ask the mask to repeat it.
If it stays dumb
claim victory.

5
Place a blindfold
on the prettiest mask.
Spin it around three times.
If it finds you
let it kiss you.

6
Place a blindfold
on yourself.
Locate a picture of a mask
by touch alone.
Pin a face on it.

7
Take a mask.
Take a friend.
Say ‘Heads or Heads?’
Listen to the call.
Flip the mask.
Decide who’s won.

8
Take a knife.
Take a mask.
Divide the mask
into four sections.
Put it back together
in the wrong order.
Think who it resembles.

9
Set eight masks
on a dining room table
with knives and forks
at the ears.
Pull the tablecloth sharply away
taking the masks with it.
Leave eight faces and silver
neatly in place.

10
Walk into an empty room.
Watch it fill up.
Talk with strangers and friends.
Remove your mask.
Ask them who you are.
Don't believe them.
Cheat.

Braille-bought Cards

Chosen for their indentations,
abrasions, their gritty glitter,
their bell and bangle shapes,
their proud-lettered feel,
they were testimony to the fact
that *Merry Christmas, Mum* was not enough.
Such sentiments would swim indecipherable
across her near-blindness
but tactile did the trick;
something to touch and enquire about.

This year, no card needed,
I miss my own annual myopia –
eyes near-closed in the card shop,
finger-tipping myself into her place,
into that nursing home, that armchair
and into those misty green eyes
unclouding to understanding
on Christmas morning.

The Casting Boat

for drowned angels
for the splash of Lucifer
for a death insurance policy

for the pitched bottle to Heaven's sweet Santa,
the skeleton key to the Kingdom,
the sweat painted veil

for one crusted thorn,
a spear and a sponge,
the floated joists of a cross

for death's shadow lit
for the uncreased shroud,
the rolled stone

for the torn bread bobbing,
the three in one,
the surface spill of blood-red wine,

the washed up doubts
for all, for most, for some of this
turned tangible, indisputable

for the one provable line in this litany
that will surface and be seen,
hooked into air and breathing

for the Thine is the Kingdom
for the power, the glory
for the ever and ever

for a netful of Amens
that are never
for ending

In the Detail

Central to this,
if not centred *in* this,
the white (the only true white) tongue
of milk at the jug's earthenware tip drools –
all of this delicate draining
caught up in the lymphatics of hands and arms,
the litany of muscle and mime.
This much and more can be seen:
basket, bread and lattice,
cap and brocade, a skirt
the colour of burgundy's residue
on an unwashed glass.
But beyond aesthetics –
beyond colour and composition,
plaster, cloth, pigment and skin,
beyond the lens of *camera obscura*,
beneath bodice, blouse and undergarment,
the unnamed knot of vessels,
the auricle, ventricle, pericardium and valve –
all is inventory, index and explanation;
all is detail and understanding;
everything is words, numbers, words:
c. 1658 – 60.
Oil on canvas.
45.4 by 40.6 cm.
Milk, pearl earring white, x centimetres
off centre.

Dita Von Teese

Dita Von Teese, Dita Von Teese
she's scarlet, a harlot, a temptress, a tease,
she's love without marriage and sex without sleaze:
milky skinned, silky skinned Dita Von Teese.

She's nobody's wife and she's nobody's squeeze
but a mistress at times to the ones who beg Please
and we're talking whips here, not birds and the bees
with the luscious, delicious Dita Von Teese.

Hot in the spot with a flourish she frees
a strap or suspender with deft expertise,
removing her stockings and basque by degrees,
the innocent, sinocent Dita Von Teese.

She's a Page torn from Bettie, she's not one of these
catwalk anorexics, all elbows and knees,
as immodest a goddess as anyone she's
the exotic, erotic Dita Von Teese.

Forget greenhouse gasses, the felling of trees;
forget C02, even Greenpeace agrees
global warming's all down to this woman 'cause she's
the sizzling, twizzling, Dita Von Teese.

Moon-gazing Hare

for Alwyn

I can't imagine he sees much,
this emerald teardrop of clay
with round eyes, pepper pot snout,
mouth carved curved in mute fascination
and ears folded back like insect wings
each side of the invisible paralysis of his spine.

Maybe not even the moon,
nightly arcing its imperfect medallion
or its pared fingernail scythe
beyond the scope of his stiff-necked stare;
certainly not the pandemonium of life
at ground level: the mower and shears,
the blown leaves, the spider and shrew.

He'll note the flit of a gnat, perhaps,
or the heavy lingering contemplation of a bee
above his eye line
but not much else, surely,
beyond the changing colour of sky,
the passing clouds, the odd star.

Yet he's transfixed
and I love his devotion to duty,
his focus, his inert attentiveness,
the way his head tilts
unflinchingly upwards to a Heaven
that ministers rain to him like eyedrops,
sun like benediction,
snow like the flakes of that moon
not yet seen
but watched for all the same.

Stereotypical

There were nowt but drippin' left when I come back from walkin' t' whippet so I give young Raymond a thick ear and told 'im not t' mek fun of 'is sister.

"But I 'aven't got a sister, dad", says he.

"Don't answer back", says I, " 'ere's sixpence. Go an' get me a *Bury Evening News* and a crate of ale and be sure t' bring back t' change."

Were t' wife who noticed *Tennyson* pokin' out from under me cloth cap.

"Bin to t' library again, I see", she says, all observant like.

Before y' could say *George Formby* she's took up book an' 'ad a ganders.

"S'pose we'll 'ave you pacin' up and down all night spoutin' poetry", she says. "Las' week ruddy Byron and now ruddy Alfred - 'alf a league, 'alf a league, 'alf a league – y'd think ruddy gramophone'd stuck."

Well, that did it.

"Stop y' yawpin', woman an' get me tea on t' table", says I. "I've bin down t' dole all mornin', sweatin' over t' dominoes in t' *Duck an' Trumpet* all afternoon an' exercisin' t' whippet up an' down back jigger all evenin'. I'll 'ave tripe an' black puddin' an' a bottle o' stout, an' let's 'ave a bit more respect for Alfred Lord, if y' don't mind."

Aye. No doubt who wears t' trousers in this 'ouse, I can tell y'.

Blow me! Next thing I know she's scarpered out t' back door wi' remains of me dole money and gone off to t' Bingo before you can say O*ur Gracie*. Lad didn't come back wi' t' paper an' ale neither.

"Well, it's me an' thee, Walter", I says, turnin' t' page 42 and to t' whippet. Partial to a bit of Classic Verse is Walter.

Bluebell Scavenger Hunt

Collect one each of the following:

a link of daisy unchained
an empty goblet of silver birch
a leaf in the shape of England's heart
a buzzard's feather sodden out of trim
a clock with blown hands
a trench of unbitten blade
the dead beneath the smothering tree
the unsplittable rowan and the pellet-eyed mouse
the weed above its station
the illusory dead dog of shadow
the one ball of unsnagged wool on barbed wire
the last bluebell of spring beneath the triptych of a fox's paw

No points will be added for noticing
the way nature, nearly left to its own devices,
roughs itself up a bit –
takes no prisoners.

Flatly Stated

We only have their word after all;
their words and their images
and you can do anything these days
with words and pictures.

I'm on the level.
So is the Earth
but people don't just twist the truth
they roll it in a ball and bounce it
so fast that you can't focus on it.

They'd have you believe the horizon
curves like the lip of a crater,
that New Zealand rolls beneath our feet
like that ball I told you about.
They'd have America at full tilt
with its skyscrapers horizontal as coat pegs;
the Sahara sands, artexed to the world and unshiftable.

They even have us moving,
revolving in space for Christ's sake!
They have their stories, their lies and their angles.
How's this for spin:
fifty-seven million of us on one convex isle
chasing continents we'll never catch?
Believe me, I know how the story truly ends
and it's in a waterfall of sea so spectacular
no barrel in the world could protect their fall.

Exploring Space

They shared a cramped romance,
a too tight love, a one size fits all.

She tested the give in it one day,
felt the stitches crack, poked an arm free.

He was too busy exhaling
to notice the rest of her following it.

Only when she'd gone, sloughed his love completely,
did he appreciate how much space there was to fill.

He thought of the positives,
saw himself a car gunning out of a chicane.

She found herself lost and enjoying it.

He turned three hundred and sixty degrees,
realised how big his life was.

She didn't turn at all for fear of seeing him again.

Spellbound

one eye open, one eye shut
a rose thorn prick, a giant's foot
a waiting wolf, a dagger's cut
one eye open, one eye shut

two steps forward, one step back
a girl in crimson, a hag in black
a lightning flash, a thundercrack
one step forward, two steps back

three iron couldrons, three dark woods
one lost princess, seven hoods
one glass empties, one stream floods
three iron couldrons, three dark woods

four paths taken, four trails lost
one troll's riddle, one bridge crossed
one deep snowfall, one Jack Frost
four trails taken, four paths lost

five towers climbed and six traps sprung
seven spells broken, eight bells rung
nine children eaten, ten mirrors hung
one tale told and one song sung

a baby crying, an empty cot
a trip to market, a witch's plot
a twig from a broomstick, a lover's knot
one eye open, one eye shut

one gold chalice, one white knight
one spiked apple, one fierce light
one glass case on one dark night
one eye open, one shut tight

His Master's Voice
for Betty

At the fag end
of the summer that wasn't,
at the dog end
of the day,
the poem I promised you
I wouldn't write
comes cloyingly puppy-eyed,
half-hearted
into the half-light.

If a theft of plums
from a fridge can be forgiven
forgive me this,
this snouting intrusion
into a poem
that should know better,
this young dog's nose,
black as a plum,
never riper, never wetter.

Softly, Softly

We are not prepared or equipped for this,
God or God-knows-who made some omission.
If only we could smell Love's threatened kiss
like scent on a warm trail, make provision
for the drill of Love's keen unflinching gaze,
feel the touch of Love's brand or cooling balm,
sense the twist of its unexpected ways,
hear the sound of its clattering alarm.
If we could train each sense to be alert
to all the tricks that Love itself might pull
and be forewarned of any pending hurt
that lurks behind a mask called 'beautiful'
then we could frisk Romance and check the score:
instead of making love, be making sure.

A Prayer for the Faithless

Time, I think, for a prayer
for those not trapped in the harp strings;
those who choose not to plait their limbs
through the wires and wear that vest like a cage.

Time, I feel, for a hymn
for those who rock in the wind of God's breath
yet won't slip over Heaven's lip; for those spiked
not speared by the Devil's forked tongue.

Time, I believe, for a sweet eternity
for the dazed, damned or undecided
who'll neither bask in gold
nor burn in brimstone

but who'll forever spin in the land of in between,
not as fretful children spin,
searching for the hand that's helping,
the face that's familiar,

but rather as dust that blows
into the eyes of Bosch and Pourbus
and, like Longinus,
makes them see.

Although not mentioned in the Bible, according to some traditions Longinus was the blind centurion who pierced Christ's side at the cross. Blood splashed into his eye from the lance and restored his sight.

Source: Groeninge Museum, Bruges

Cause and Effect

Forget, if you will, the old familiar tale
of a butterfly's wing beating up a hurricane
on the other side of the earth
and consider more tangible miracles:
the raking claws of a grubbing badger
felling an oak, the bluebells for bedding
he brings for his mate
and the tick that rides her harlequin pelt
as if it were the prairie of the world

and of the flowers themselves,
those fairy mob caps
with their delicate details
printed on a tissue thin wind,
think of them beneath the hulk
and scrub of her haunches
and of the blue confetti
of her waking and shaking

and of the oak too, rolling with bugs,
its raised starfish roots
cradling a cabbage white
with wings in mid-beat,
a tidal wave just begun,
a raindrop just about to.

Acknowledgments

Acknowledgements are due to the editors of the following publications in which some of these poems first appeared: *Beyond the Cloister, The Coffee House, Edinburgh Review, In the Red, iota, Patchwork, Poems for Peace, Poetry Pool, tex'ture, The Ugly Tree, UniVerse, Weyfarers.*

Carry on Listening was commissioned by Cheshire County Council for the 'Carry on Listening' project for people with learning difficulties.

Identity was written for Ellesmere Port & Neston Borough Council's 'Fusion' project, 'Our Town'.

A Man of Letters was written for the 'Dr. Samuel Johnson Tercentenary Project'.

Other books by John Lindley

House of Wonders (Riverdane, 2008)
Cheshire Rising (Cheshire County Council, 2005)
Scarecrow Crimes (New Hope International, 2002)
Stills From November Campaigns (Tarantula, 1998).
Cages and Fields (1982)
Pacific Envelope (1976)

Cover illustration: *Cast Your Net Again* by Daniel Bonnell.
Further information on the artist can be found on
www.BonnellArt.com